I0758420

Woman, Life, Freedom

Poems of an uprising

Lida Berghuis

Illustrations by Natasha Berghuis

Dedication

It's been a year since Mahsa was brutally killed for breaking rules that are limiting the freedom of the women of Iran.

It's been forty years since ten other brave women gave their lives because they were not willing to recant their beliefs in equality of men and women and other matters dealing with justice and harmony in society. These ten Bahá'í women were given the choice to deny their faith or die by hanging. They chose the latter. The youngest, Mona, was seventeen. Nosrat Ghufrani Yaldaie was forty-six. She was my Bahá'í Sunday School teacher when I was thirteen and still lived in Shíráz, Iran. She was a woman of conviction and faith and she gave of her time to serve the community.

It's been seventy-one years since Táhirih was strangled because she thought a new day had dawned and women and men needed to be treated equality and have the same freedoms.

I dedicate this book of poems to these women and others who have given their lives to further the cause of the equality of women and men.

Table of Contents

Preface

Growing up in Iran in the 1970's, I was fully aware that women had less freedom than men. Parents felt they should protect their girl-children from the ills of society and that meant restricting their attendance in social activities. At that time, some women wore headscarves or chadors (veils) but these women lived in villages or belonged to conservative families. A few of my classmates in high school wore headscarves, but, most of the girls and women that I was in contact with did not wear any. I saw the requirement of wearing headscarves as a dictate of the clerics and not something to do with Islam. The reasons I heard about why women should cover their hair did not make sense to me. I didn't see it as a sign of modesty. I didn't think it would stop men from being tempted. I felt men have more self-control than that or should have. I saw covering one's hair as a relic of the past, something that did not have a place in modern society.

One of the heroines of the Bahá'í Faith is Táhirih, an erudite woman as well as a poet, who wanted to change the way women were seen and treated. At a time when women covered their faces in the presence of men, and she had to speak to other men who wanted to listen to her talks from behind a curtain, she walked into a gathering of men without her face-covering (niqab). This was to symbolize the fact that in this new religion the equality of women and men was established, new laws were coming into being and women need no longer cover their face and hair. Her actions caused a commotion in the gathering of course and shocked the men who were present. Bahá'í women gradually gave up wearing the headscarf and the veil. They were encouraged to receive a good eduction and work in all professions alongside men.

This view of women was very important for me. I went to an American primary school and was quite aware of the fact that Western women had much more freedom and many more opportunities in society. That sort of freedom and those opportunities were what I longed for.

Táhirih was eventually killed at the age of 36 because she was promoting a new religion and a new way of thinking. When they killed her, she said, "You can kill me as soon as you like but you cannot stop the emancipation of women"*.
I always looked up to Táhirih as a symbol of women's freedom and equality.

My family left Iran just before the Islámic revolution when I was 14. When I heard that the wearing of the head scarf had become mandatory in Iran, I was quite upset. How could a few men decide what millions of women should do? Women who resisted wearing headscarves could be arrested, fined, or jailed. A new force, called the morality police, came into being. These individuals had to make sure the new directives regarding how women were to dress in public would be obeyed. The treatment women without headscarves received was belittling, aggressive and unjust. Excessive force was used in arresting these women, and they were often sentenced to a number of lashes and prison time.

I watched these developments from Canada, where we now lived, and was happy I did not have to deal with these restrictions. I don't know what I would have done had I lived in Iran at that time. I'm sure I would feel very rebellious and try to avoid obeying this new law. Nevertheless, I'm sure I would not have had much choice.

The women of Iran started protesting the wearing of the headscarves when it became a law. They demonstrated in the streets, disobeyed the law, and of course paid a heavy price for it. In 2017, a women's rights activist, Masih Alinejad, launched the White Wednesdays' campaign. On this day, women were encouraged not to wear a headscarf or wear white clothing as a sign of their opposition to mandatory hijab and share videos of themselves.

In September of 2022, something happened that made women even more determined to get rid of this oppressive law. It was the death of Mahsa Amini while she was in police custody for not wearing her headscarf properly. This twenty-two-year-old was probably hit on the head so hard that later she went into a coma and died. Following that, large demonstrations happened in the streets and the anthem of Woman, Life, Freedom was born. An uprising led by women got underway. Men joined the women too. They had their own grievances, economic, political, and otherwise. Three months of demonstrations ensued and around 500 young Persians, some as young as 10 or 16 were killed in the process of quelling this uprising. Eventually, tens of thousands of people were arrested and jailed, and a few were put to death following sham trials. The street demonstrations decreased over time, but women continued to fight the mandatory wearing of the hijab. They posted videos of themselves without headscarves and dancing in public, another activity that is not permitted for women in Iran.

As if to avenge the actions of young schoolgirls who protested against the hijab as well, poisonous gases were released in girls' schools nations wide, making the students nauseous and sending many to hospitals. The government did nothing to find and arrest those involved. They turned a blind eye to this atrocity.

The Persians outside Iran have been very supportive of the cause of the Iranian women and the other demonstrators and have held numerous rallies across Europe and North America. The news of the uprising is being covered by Persian news channels outside Iran as well as the Western media. In Iran, however, the government-sanctioned radio and TV tell their own version of the story and call the demonstrators "the enemy". The government wants to stifle this movement at any price.

I started writing poems about the uprising in Iran and the situation of women there in September of 2022 when Mahsa

Amini was killed, and the demonstrations started. Initially, I thought regime change would come to Iran very soon, but that didn't happen. However, it is clear that there is an awakening in the psyche of the people of Iran that will ultimately lead to freedom and equality. The question is when. Perseverance, courage, collaboration, and unity will lead to the success of this movement and the Persians inside and outside Iran seem eager to see this uprising to its conclusion.

The issue of hijab and how women dress has become very intertwined with the viability of the current regime. Those in power feel if they become lenient in this area, people will ask for other freedoms as well and their hold on power will weaken. The morality police, members of which arrested Mahsa, has been disbanded, but women who don't wear head scarves are still targeted. At the same time, videos of women without headscarves in Iran is all over the internet. Women remain defiant and won't back down. Not wearing the headscarf is only one of the demands of the women. They want equal treatment as well. Right now, there are many discriminatory laws against women in Iran. These inequalities exist in laws dealing with divorce, marriage, inheritance, and child custody. I admire the courage of the women in Iran and hope that they will achieve their goals soon. After all, if women are allowed to fully engage in society, the whole society will benefit. This is not just a women's issue.

*God Passes By, p.75

Woman, Life, Freedom

Woman, Life, Freedom
Zan, Zendegi, Azadi
The cry of not only women
But also men who support them
Because lifting up women
Will lift up society
Which includes men
Women are centre stage
Women lead
And when women lead
Things are bound to change
Their passion, their conviction
The wrongs they have suffered
Have fanned the flames
Flames that are spreading like wildfire
And burning the structures that have
Tried to keep them in their place

September 2022

Tears of the world

Tears run down the cheeks of the world
Her brow is knotted with anguish
Another injustice
This time against a young woman who was innocent
Why did she have to die?

How long will these tribulations last?
When will equality and justice return?
When will the pain that is felt be alleviated?
When will joy come back?

I think the road ahead is long
Change doesn't happen overnight
But we must keep our hopes up
We must march on despite the trials

We must focus on the good that is happening
Work for the betterment of our community
Collaborate with like-minded people
And stay steadfast until freedom is achieved

September 18, 2022

For Mahsa Amini, who was arrested
for breaking the dress code set for women
in the Islámic Republic of Iran,
and who died in police custody

At issue

Women, wronged for so many years
Women, restricted
Women
The world sees you in the streets
The world sees you burning your scarves
The world sees men also fighting for your rights

At issue
A dress code that has been imposed on you
A dress code that you have fought till now
A dress code that has nothing to do with modesty
A dress code for which you have been arrested and harmed

At issue
Equality in all areas
At issue
Your dignity being respected
At issue
Your right to freedom

Courageous women
I see your hair flowing in the wind
I see your clothes being your choice
I see your future as bright
I see you triumphant in time

September 22, 2022

Sun of justice

The difference is their conviction
The difference is their ardour and being on the side of justice
The difference is that they are not obeying anyone
This is their fight
They are the soldiers and the generals

A fire has been lit for freedom
Its flames are growing every day
The winds of opposition only cause it to spread
You can't control a wildfire

The energy of youth
Youth who are tired of lies
Youth who know their rights are being trampled on
Youth who feel they have nothing to lose
This energy feeds the fire

Injustice can prevail for a while
It can maintain its strong grip on power for some time
But those who are tired of corruption and empty promises
Those who long for freedom and equality
They can only be suppressed so long

The night of oppression is dark
But we can see the glimpses of the dawn
A dawn that will come because of the sacrifices being made
A dawn that will have its price
But soon will the sun of justice shine

September 26, 2022

For the young protesters in the streets of Iran

Freedom fighters

My brain needs a break
From the bad news and the good news
My brain needs a break
From all the emotions that they evoke
All the expectations and hopes

But those who are fighting don't get a break
They are in the streets every day
They are sending their videos every night
They cannot afford to rest or take a break

The work of a freedom fighter is not for the faint of heart
They raise their voices for change
They sacrifice, they get injured, they get arrested

I can take a break from the news here
When it becomes overwhelming
But they can't

September 28, 2022

Equality

What do the women of Iran want?
Equality!
What does that mean?
To be treated with respect and dignity
And to participate in all arenas of society
Women want to wear what they want
And not be controlled in the name of Islam
They want to feel the wind in their hair
They want the end of the separation of women and men
everywhere
They don't want to be told what they can and can't do
They want an end to the harassment they have long endured

October 8, 2022

Dawn of a new day

It's an explosion of pent-up anger
It's a cry from deep within their souls
It's having been controlled for years
And now smelling the sweet scent of freedom

It's wonderful
It's inspiring
It's the dawn of a new day

It's the energy of youth
Their desire for change
Their confidence in what they can do

It's solidarity
People from all walks of life
Young, old, poor, and wealthy
Women, men, artists, and athletes

The march to freedom gathers momentum every day
People around the world send their well wishes
Women cut their hair in the memory of Mahsa
And so many young lives that were sacrificed

It's a new dawn
A new day
And the future looks bright

October 9, 2022

My heart aches

My heart aches for the people of Iran
For the young boys and girls in the streets
Who sacrifice their freedom and sometimes their lives
Standing up for what they believe in

Their hearts are on fire
Their rage against injustice fuels their actions
They know their rights
They know they are deprived of them
And they can no longer stay quiet

It breaks my heart that speaking up for their rights
Can lead to their death in my country of birth
That these young lives are snuffed out so cruelly and easily
As if their existence matters not

I feel deeply for the values they are fighting for
Covering one's hair is not a sign of modesty
Why should women hide their beautiful hair from view?
All the excuses that are given are just that, excuses
Behind these dictates, is the desire to subjugate women
And these things are as clear as daylight to the youth of Iran

These brave girls who die for lighting their head scarves on
fire
Will be remembered long into the future
Their lives will be celebrated, and their courage will be
lauded
Years after those who jailed them or killed them are gone and
forgotten

October 10, 2022

Never lose hope

For years, I've been wondering when freedom will return to
Iran
When women will be able to choose how they dress
themselves
When they can freely and without fear walk in the streets
When they will not be considered the weaker sex
When their contributions to society inside and outside the
home will be celebrated
When they can bike and swim and sing and dance
When they can voice their opinions and be listened to
It's been years…
From time to time, I've seen signs of hope
And then my hopes have been dashed
Now, I'm hopeful again
And I think to myself
I will return to Iran one day
And on that day, wearing the headscarf will no longer be
mandatory
Women will show their lovely hair
And laugh and sing with joy about the freedom that has been
so long in coming

October 11, 2022

Extraordinary times

These are extraordinary times
These are days of solidarity
When people put their lives on the line
For freedom of thought
For dignity
For truthfulness
For justice
For equality

These are unprecedented times
When the young and the old are united
And speak with one voice

These are terrible times
When young people and children are sacrificed to uphold an
ideology
The price they are paying is very high
The grief their parents and their supporters feel is immense
But their blood will water the plant of freedom

These are hopeful times
Because a nation has come together
Discovered the power there is in unity
And is marching on a path that leads to freedom

These are important times
The world has heard the cry of the people of Iran
And is arising in solidarity and protesting in the streets
To ensure the freedom of the people of this land

These are formative times
A new system based on respect for all
Based on diversity of thought and belief
Based on fundamental human rights
Is being forged

These are extraordinary times
Women are in the forefront of change
Their valour is on display
They are tired of the status quo
They are the freedom fighters of today

October 12, 2022

She was every woman

She was every woman
She could be me
She could be you
She was not political
She was a visitor, a guest
Is that how one treats a guest?
Is that how one treats a sister or a mother?

She was every woman
And she was killed senselessly
She was killed in a most cruel manner
She was killed with a lot of anger
Why?
Because she was a woman
And did not closely follow the unreasonable dictates of the
regime

She was every woman
And she was killed brutally
She awakened again the anger that has been smouldering for
years
She brought the people into the streets
Demanding freedom, equality, a normal life
And a future they could look forward to

She was every woman
And she will be remembered in history
As one whose death started a revolution

October 13, 2022

For Mahsa Amini

Wildfire

The events are happening so fast
Yet painfully slow
Because each day people are being arrested, injured and
killed
Each day families don't know where their loved ones are
Each day they worry for their safety

We are in the middle of a revolution
It's gone past demonstrations
It's gone past demands
It's a revolution a long time in coming

There were demonstrations in the past
People made demands
They were arrested and jailed
And things seemed to go back to 'normal'
But under that illusive 'normal', embers were burning
The rage continued
The discontent continued
It seemed to have been controlled
But it would erupt again
Once again victory would seem within their grasp
Yet again they would face the wrath of those in power
And the fire would die down

This time the fire has spread far and wide
It's a wildfire that is out of control
Yes, they are trying to put the fire out
But this time it's different
People have risen up
And won't stop till they achieve their goal

October 13, 2022

Hear me roar

I am woman, hear me roar
Hear me cry out with the pent-up anger of years
Hear me shout the anthem of freedom
Hear me voice my grievances
It's been long enough
And I'm tired of being told who I should be

I am woman, hear me roar
With the courage of a lioness
Prepared to fight for her home
Prepared to protect her kin
With fervour and ferocity

I am woman, hear me roar
Don't expect me to be quiet any longer
Don't try to control me because it does not work
A sense of justice has been awakened within me
Which can set fire to injustice and brutality

I am woman, hear me roar
I am stronger than you think
When I want to defend my rights
I am an opponent you should fear

I am woman, hear me roar:
Woman, Life, Freedom

October 15, 2022

A child

A child has died
No, children have died
And why, you may ask
Because they spoke their minds
Asked for their rights
Took off their scarves
Fought for freedom

And this is a real fight
Many have died
Innocent ones
At the hands of brutal people
Whose hearts seem to be made of stone
Who are willing to kill their own countrymen

People are dying in the streets
This is not an easy fight
Courage is needed
Anger fuels their cause
But why should children die?

October 15, 2022

Smoke billows

Smoke billows from the prison on the hill
A thick grey column has risen to the sky
It marks the place of atrocities and injustices
Rounds of shots can be heard
Who is being killed and why?

Explosions can be seen
Tear gas is being fired on those who have nowhere to hide
The injured are being taken away
But why have they been injured in the first place?

These are dark days
And dark acts of hatred are being committed
These days are being marked with people chanting
With cars honking
With headscarves burning
With placards and signs
With grievances being written on walls

These days are dark
But they will not last
People have passed through the valley of fear
They cannot be stopped
And they will continue to ask for their rights
And one bright morning, the sun of justice will shine

October 16, 2022

Fire in a prison in Karaj

What I say

You say I should cover my hair and body
So I don't tempt men
I say men should be and are stronger than that
You say the headscarf is a sign of modesty
I say it's a means of control
You say dancing excites the other sex
I say dancing brings joy into my life
You say women's singing voice shouldn't be heard
I say you are depriving society of so much
You say women are the weaker sex
And they need protection
I say you haven't seen what we are capable of
You say the place of women is at home
I say society needs our contribution
You hit, and arrest and try to torture women into submission
I say this cruelty is much worse than what you consider
immodesty
You do these things in the name of religion
I say religion is for peace
You fear women it seems
And you should
Because women are strong and courageous
And will fight for equality like lionesses
Until they achieve their goal

October 17, 2022

Unity

The hallmark of this movement is unity
Unity between the university students and their professors
Unity between the *Turk* and *Lur* and *Bakhtiari*
Unity between the less fortunate and the affluent
Unity between workers and society
Unity among the students in high schools
Unity among the people marching in the streets

This is unprecedented in Iran
This revolution has a beating heart
That of valiant women and girl-children
This revolution has momentum
It's a movement that cannot be stopped
The dam has broken and it can't be shut

I salute the women and girls of Iran
I salute the university students and professors
I salute the workers who are on strike
I salute the businesspeople who close their shops
I salute those who walk around without their headscarves

This road may be long
Many lives are being sacrificed
Many are spending their time in captivity
But there is no turning back
The world is watching in admiration
And I pray and hope that the dawn is near

October 18, 2022

The youth of Iran

The fervour of these youth
The anger of these youth
Their fists raised up in the air
Their hearts full of hope

These youth are speaking up for freedom
They are tired of being told lies
They want a different future
And they are sacrificing their lives

The passion of these youth
Throwing away their scarves
Showing what was hidden
For years now

These youth are being arrested
They are dying
Because they want a different life
Because they are no longer afraid to speak up

I'm proud of these youth
I honor their cause
I stand with them
Until there is freedom
I'm awe-struck with their bravery
Climbing walls without headscarves*

I'm not paying a price with my life
Or with my imprisonment
I can only speak up with my pen
With my fists in the air

October 19, 2022

*A climber who didn't wear a headscarf
 In an international competition

My beautiful locks

If I entice you with my beautiful locks
Which is a gift from God to adorn my face
The problem is you, not me

If my bare ankles arouse in you sensual thoughts
The problem is you, not me

My natural body is to be celebrated, not hidden
Would you cover up a bouquet of roses because it's too beautiful?
Close your eyes instead!

Close your eyes if the price of your lustful thoughts
Is my imprisonment under layers of cloth

Close your eyes if you can't handle God-given beauty
And sexualize what is natural and part of life

Close your eyes
Don't put me in bondage because of your weaknesses
Close your eyes

November 4, 2022

Indomitable spirit

Physical violence won't subdue the spirit of these freedom
fighters
The wounds they suffer will not weaken their resolve
Their spirits are strong
You can pummel their flesh
You can shoot at their bodies
But they will rise up stronger the next time

November 6, 2022

It's a marathon

It's a marathon
Sometimes a bloody one unfortunately
Sacrifices are being made with lives lost or imprisonment
But the energy of the youth propelling this movement is
endless
Their idealism and hope for change fuels their cause
They want better lives
They are done with the status quo
They plan and organize
They march and they chant
And they cannot be beaten into submission

These youth have attracted the attention of the world
People in Germany, UK, Sweden, and South America
Have heard their anthem of freedom
Artists are singing their song
The world is watching
Persians overseas and others are walking with the people of
Iran
This is a just cause
The demands are simple: Woman, Life, Freedom

November 6, 2022

Nobility

If they don't treat women well
It doesn't bode well for the rest of society
If they don't treat religious minorities well
They will eventually denigrate other groups as well

The thinking that sees one group as better than others
Eventually will see everyone else as other
Only those in power will be immune to oppression

Let's stand up not just for our own rights
But the rights of every marginalized group in society
This is the sign of nobility

November 7, 2022

They persist

I look and listen from a distance
And see a nation in turmoil and pain
People asking for justice and equality
Asking for a normal and acceptable quality of life
But change does not come easily
There is always resistance and pushback

Nevertheless, the clock cannot be turned back
People are no longer content with the status quo
They continue to speak up
Despite the crackdowns
Despite the threats
Despite the imprisonments
And despite the executions

I admire the strength and courage
Of my countrymen and women
I worry for their safety and security
And I look forward to the day when their sacrifices will have
paid off
And peace, security and equality prevail

January 6, 2023

Sad faces

I look at your faces and I feel sadness, shock, anger and
disbelief
I cannot imagine the grief of your family and friends
One of you had already lost your mother and father
Now the world is your family
Your innocent and youthful faces
Have been broadcast in the media internationally
Your sacrifice has not gone unnoticed

January 8, 2023

For two of the demonstrators who were hanged

What is the secret of this song?

What is the secret of this song?
Why did it touch so many hearts?
Why did it become the anthem for a movement?
Why was it worthy of winning a prize?

The song was a cry for freedom
Freedom from nonsensical restrictions
Freedom to express oneself
Freedom from oppressive rules

The words of this song expressed the desires of a people
People who have suffered for so long
People who are beaten for how they dress
People who are jailed for what they say

The lyrics of this song expressed what was needed
To show the world what was happening in Iran
The days of carrying out injustices without others knowing is
over
What is happening is laid bare for all to see

The words that bubbled up from the soul of a young man
Have reached the world
The song has been sung everywhere
The truth has been heard
This is the secret of this song

February 2023

For Shirvin's song, Baraye (For)

Gold stars

You got seven years?
That's like seven gold stars
For your efforts to serve your country and community

You got ten years?
That's like ten gold stars
For your efforts in the arena of equality

You got 17 years?
That's like 17 gold stars
They must be really threatened by you
Seventeen years is the sign of anger and revenge
Seventeen years is to prevent others from following in your
footsteps

Prisons have become the gatherings places
Of those who do good deeds
It used to be the opposite
But we are living in the end of times
And things are no longer as they used to be
Prison sentences are a badge of honour

February 22, 2023

What we want

What we want is an ordinary life
We don't ask for much
Just allow us to wear what we want
What's the harm in that?
Just allow us to speak freely
What are you afraid of?
Just allow us these normal things
Safety in the streets
Practicing our religion
Equality regardless of ethnicity
Just treat women like you treat men
This is the 21st century
The old ways of looking at the world do not work
Old rules and laws do not suit our society
What we ask for are simple things
Let us breathe!

February 25, 2023

I say no!

You want me to cover my hair
I say no!
You say it's the sign of piety
I say no!
You say it will protect me from harm
I say no!
You say otherwise I'll excite men
I say no!
You can't convince me to do something I don't want to do
You don't realize how strong I am
You have tried to put me down
But each time you see me rise
You fear me and my courage
You should!
I'm determined and won't back down
I will continue this fight
Woman, Life, Freedom

March 3, 2023

Girl-children

Girl-children are being poisoned
Why?
Because they fear them
They fear their strength of character
They fear their desire for equality
They fear their resolve to achieve it
Why else would they poison them?

Young girls have shown how powerful they are
How determined they are
How fearless they are
How disruptive of the norms of the regime they are
How united they are

This poisoning will only strengthen their resolve
It will bring their cause to the world
It will show the cruelty of those in power
And how low they will go to achieve their goals

The day is near that all these atrocities will come to an end
When those responsible will be prosecuted
When justice and equality will return to our land
And Woman, Life, Freedom will prevail

March 4, 2023

About systematic poisoning of girl-children at schools

Girl-children poisoned

Girl-children are being poisoned
A gender is under attack
Girls who can't defend themselves
This is a terrorist act
It's an act of revenge
On those who dared to speak up
It is a cowardly act
Preying on those who can't respond
These actions will lead to the demise
Of those who perpetrate them
These are the flailing arms
Of one who's about to drown

March 5, 2023

Can I be angry?

Can I be angry at injustice and ignorance?
Or should I be demure and stay quiet?
Should I not rock the boat?
And why not?
Things won't get done if we stay quiet
A little bit of courage goes a long way
But mostly I feel frustrated at the slow rate of progress
We live in the 21st century
And we see behaviour that belongs to a thousand years ago
Have we not advanced and developed?
Have we not adopted new ways of thinking?
The equality of women and men is an established fact now
It's not fully in practice of course
But girls' education should not be a question any longer
How do we want society to thrive
If half of its members are held back?
What are those in power afraid of?
Or who are they afraid of?
Women?
A time will come when this kind of thinking will be ancient
history
Men will realize that uplifting women will uplift the society
they live in
Don't we want educated mothers to raise our children?
I am angry at the injustices and ignorance I see!

March 6, 2023

Five Thousand girls

Five thousand girl victims
No, they are not hysterical
No, this is not things being blown out of proportion
No, it's not a negative campaign of the social media
Please acknowledge it for what it is
A terrorist act
On a widespread scale
At places of learning
On those who comprise half of the population
Poisoning girl-children is an act to be ashamed of
It's cowardly
The world is watching
These tactics will only fan the flames of the uprising
They are doomed to failure
Only small minds find solutions like this
And as a result, so many suffer

March 7, 2023

For the girls being poisoned with gas at their schools

Every day should be women's day

Every day should be women's day
After all they are our mothers, sisters, and daughters
After all it's women who raise the next generation
They sacrifice their ease and comfort
They are the glue that keeps the family united
They are strong in times of turmoil
They are compassionate and patient

What can men do to show women their appreciation?
Treat them like they want to be treated
See them as equals in decision making
Support them so they can achieve their potential
Appreciate all the sacrifices they make
Acknowledge their important role in educating children
Give them the attention they deserve
Listen to them when they want to talk
Treat them as equals in relationships
And respect them as partners in their lives

Happy International Women's Day!

March 8, 2023

My voice

You don't want to see my hair
You don't want to hear my voice either
Expressing my opinions and asking for my rights frightens
you
You want to silence me
Me, half of the population
Me, the mother of your children
Me, your sister, and daughter
And why?
Are you afraid of the power of women?
Are you weary of us asking for our basic rights?
Women cannot be silenced
Girls cannot be poisoned into submission
Everything you do to take their rights away
Will backfire
The world is watching
These tactics don't work any longer
They will increase the anger of the population
The day will come
When we will sing and dance in the streets
And take our proper place in society
Woman, Life, Freedom

March 10, 2023

Where is the logic?

If your headscarf falls off your hair
Or even worse, you remove it in disdain
What will befall our society?
What will come of your piety?
People are hungry?
Pull your headscarf on
There is rampant corruption?
Tighten the knot
There is inflation?
Take your makeup off
Girls are being poisoned?
That's the result of them being unwise
The country is falling apart?
It's OK as long as women stay home
The economy is in shambles?
Who says women need to work?
Sister, pull your headscarf up
Without that, all is lost

March 19, 2023

As spoken by some religious leaders

My hair

Are you telling me that a few strands of hair arouse men?
I don't buy that
I say it's a power grab
It's a way of controlling half of the population
Restricting them
Putting them in their places
Clipping their wings
Muffling their voices
And what gives you the right to do that?
Who authorized you?
And why should that be the law for those who don't believe?
It's a power grab
It's demeaning
It's belittling
And women won't stand for it
The brave women of Iran are fighting back
There is no turning back
They have sacrificed so much
They have given their lives
How can they turn back?

March 27, 2023

No to headscarves

Politicians try to punish women
Who don't follow the rules of hijab set for them
Many women are refusing to wear their headscarves in the
streets
Or on the buses
Sometimes other women taunt them
Sometimes men
There can be fines
They could be arrested
But they remain defiant
They have turned a page
And won't look back
Their courage is admirable
They refuse to give in to unjust laws
Women without headscarves
Are another symbol of this uprising
To achieve freedom

April 28, 2023

Prisons in Iran

Prisons are usually a place to house people who are
dangerous to society
In Iran, that is the case as well
But Iranian prisons are now home to people who are
dangerous to the regime:
Writers who criticize
Environmental activists who tell it as they see it
Members of religious minorities
Those who oppose the government
Those who take part in peaceful protests
Those who lead these protests
Prisons have become the gathering place of
Those who want change and are not afraid to talk

April 28, 2023

Forty-four years

Poems for 44 years of struggle
Poems from the heart
Poems against injustice
Poems to lift women up
Women of Iran are standing up for their rights
And fighting with all their might
Showing their courage to the world
Iranians outside Iran are on their side
They march and ask for change as well
These battles will continue until the war is won

April 29, 2023

A year has passed

A year has passed since Mahsa was killed
This innocent daughter of Iran
It's been a year since the protests started
It's been a year since the government responded
With cruelty and violence to these protests
It's been a year since the movement of Woman, Life,
Freedom was born
It's been a year of burning headscarves
Shouting from the rooftops
Marches in the streets
And messages on the walls
It's been a year since five-hundred Iranians were killed
Because they asked for their rights
A year in which twenty-five thousand protesters were arrested
And many executions took place
These sacrifices will not be in vain
The blood of those killed will water the tree of freedom

August 2023

By the same author:

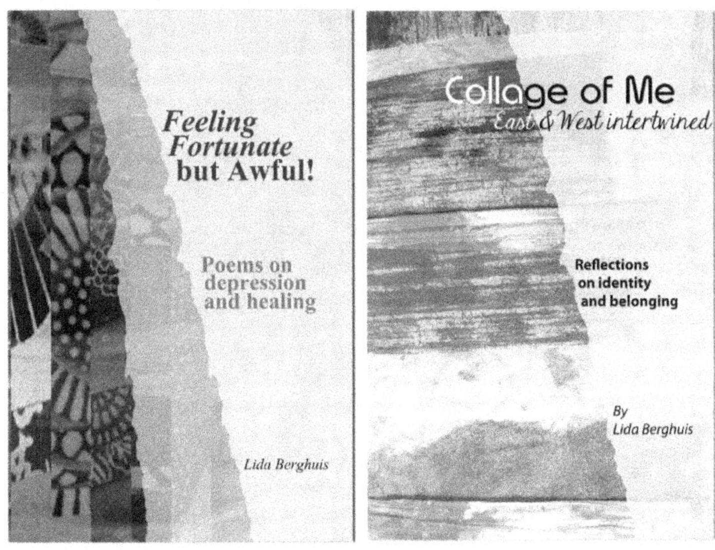

www.lidasmusings.com

55

9 798885 378262 4